THE JOY OF HEAVEN 3

Homeward Bound

Advantage
BOOKS
www.advbookstore.com

Written and Illustrated by

Daniel Leske

"...they shall MOUNT up with wings as eagles..." Isaiah 40:31

The Joy of Heaven 3: Homeward Bound by Daniel Leske
Copyright © 2014 by Daniel Leske
All Rights Reserved.
ISBN: 978-1-59755-256-1

Published by: ADVANTAGE BOOKS™
Longwood, Florida, USA
www.advbookstore.com

Library of Congress Catalog Number: 2014951372

First Printing: October 2014
14 15 16 17 18 19 20   10 9 8 7 6 5 4 3 2 1
Printed in the United States of America

By writing this book, I knew the Lord had to open the door into heaven for this story to be written! As you read it, I believe that you'll be inspired by the beauty of heaven and the specialness to it!

Wings are a very special part of heaven!

Felicia is about 8 or 9 years old in stature and Wee Angel is diminutive, like her name.

I tried to paint a picture so that you can envision it!

Each person may see and feel the experience differently. As the writer, I feel that I accomplished what I set out to do!

Always remember that the Lord is the guide.

Now go with me through that doorway ------ the doorway into heaven. I hope you enjoy the story!

List of Some of the Characters

Main characters from The Joy of Heaven 1 and 2 are Wee Angel, Felicia, Sir William, Annie, Tuddley Teddy, Lord God and Jesus.

Some of the characters in The Joy of Heaven 3 are:

Angel Gabriella and Daniella	Identical twin angels.
Toby	A St. Bernard dog with wings.
Gloria	A beautiful pelican.
Angel Rebecca	Angelic guide of the mansions.
Angel Micah	One of the power angels.
Matthew	One of the disciples.
Mark	One of the disciples.
Power riders and white winged horses	Part of the Lord's army.

Also many angels and saints that are all part of God's kingdom!

Chapter 1

Another Good Heavenly Day

After all the greetings and hugs, Wee Angel, Felicia, Sir William, and Tuddley Teddy, walked on the Lord's golden pathway, on more of this, the joy of heaven!

"The Lord said I should take you to more places in heaven and so that's what we are going to do!" said Wee Angel.

It wasn't long that five children came toward the Lord's city. They wanted to be on Sir William's back and on Tuddley Teddy's back. Wee Angel and Felicia helped them to do this. Their names were Gregg, Corey, Martin, Rachel, and Tiffany.

They visited awhile in heaven's time, reflecting over some of the places they had been in heaven.

The children definitely gave Tuddley and Sir William enough hugs! Needless to say, the two loved it and enjoyed every moment!

Within heaven's time, they said their good days and everyone was on their way.

The children were singing in the Lord's city at a praise service.

As they walked, there were some hills on both sides of the golden road.

They were gentle rolling hills. They knew that they had to fly soon, yet they wanted to spend some time with Tuddley Teddy.

So they walked, yet looked back to the Lord's city and enjoyed every step because of the beautiful glories from it.

They again looked at what they could see, because of the hills and the light at the Lord's city, which was at times very intense. So to see it at a distance, when one couldn't see the city, one could still enjoy the glories of it.

These were the different light rays and colors of it as they went into the heavenly skies.

They walked until they came to an orchard of again apples, peaches, pears, even some vines of watermelons.

"Watermelons! Oh look at them, Tuddley!" spoke up Felicia.

"Just what Tuddley loves." added Wee Angel.

They went off the golden path unto the grass. There, Wee Angel and Felicia got Tuddley a big melon.

He ate it with relish. Felicia and Wee Angel enjoyed some too!

It was a good time to rest on heaven's carpet and so they enjoyed the moment! They did that!

So! All rested, with Tuddley who found a fruit tree, with a limb not too high for his spot. He rested! Felicia and Wee Angel found places on the grass next to some irises. After heavens time Wee Angel went over to Tuddley to wake him.

He did come down from the tree, not always easy, even on heavenly bears.

Both took their turns sitting on Tuddley's back. They flew around him and played with Tuddley. This time was special to both Wee Angel and Felicia.

Wee Angel said, "We are going to have to fly so we'll leave Tuddley here."

"He's so special to us, Wee Angel!" Felicia added.

Tuddley wiggled all over!

Again, they said their good days, with more hugs.

It was always hard to part ways with Tuddley, since he had become so much a part of their friendship. Wee Angel flew around him and around him!

They sang some songs to Tuddley. Nice songs, friendship songs! Tuddley loved it.

He even got up on his back legs, for them. Tuddley was so special to them, as they knew he was special to other saints and children in heaven.

Soon both Wee Angel and Felicia flew up on the back of Sir William.

He placed his head by Tuddley Teddy too! They sort of rubbed heads, that was their way of showing good days!

He majestically opened his mighty wings and soon they were in the heavenly skies above Tuddley. Sir William circled Tuddley.

"We'll see you again, Tuddley!" both Wee Angel and Felicia called to him.

They waved and then they were on their way to a special place in heaven.

Wee Angel whispered into Sir William's ears and off he flew to it.

Chapter 2

Angel Gabriella, Angel Daniella and Toby

Sir William flew upwards now above the heavenly lands, passed over trees, hills and between hillsides.

Wee Angel said to Felicia, "We are going to another place. It's a very long ways, so William is going to fly faster than normal and longer too!"

Fly he did! Fly he did! Flying on and on and on and on... !

Both Wee Angel and Felicia were safe on the back of Sir William. They enjoyed what they saw as he flew across these lands.

In time, they saw on the horizon the area of this place with many extra glories above the area.

There were some forested hills, so they landed at the edge of them on the golden pathway. It was an area between the heavenly lands of flowers with streams and the hills. Again, they went upward into these hills with trees that were so straight up and down!

They walked and enjoyed the bushes along the golden way.

"These bushes have so many flowers on them!" said Felicia.

They enjoyed the flowers on the bushes. Many of the flowers were multicolored!

"I think that Lord God was out here with his paint brush the way these bushes look! They look so beautiful. Thank you Lord for them." Felicia added.

They enjoyed the birds, cardinals, and even a few sea gulls in the area. More doves flew as well with some owls close by them and other birds of the forest.

Both walked, whistled, and sang songs to the Lord.

Ahead of them two angels were walking, approaching closer to them. Between the angels was a large Bernard dog. The dog saw and knew Wee Angel and Sir William. He immediately came running towards them. The Bernard dog was the same as the St. Bernard dog on earth.

Wee Angel shouted, "Oh Toby! How are you! Felicia, that's Toby coming towards us!"

Toby got closer and closer. Sir William was whinnying, for he knew Toby too! The two angels then started to fly closer to them.

Wee Angel giggled, and Felicia was all smiles, as she said, "Oh what a beautiful dog!"

Toby was now close to them with Wee Angel and Felicia giving him all the hugs they could!

The two angels were now there too! One of them flew up on Sir William's back. The other angel was hugging Sir William.

Quickly Felicia noticed they both looked identical. They were twins. They both had beautiful deep golden brown hair.

One angel said, "I'm Angel Gabriella and this is Angel Daniella."

Angel Daniella spoke, "We are so glad to meet both of you."

Wee Angel said, "I'm Wee Angel and this is Felicia."

Felicia said, "I'm so glad to meet you and Toby too!"

Again the angels were a little larger than Wee Angel.

Jubilation was there.

Felicia with giggles said, "Wee Angel, Toby has wings. Look! Look at the wings, he's got!"

Again Toby was another animal of heaven with wings. Wee Angel was now sitting on Toby's back.

Wee Angel asked Gabriella if it was all right for Toby to come with Felicia and her. Wee Angel said they could see him later! Both agreed, it was all right!

Wee Angel said, "When we go, I'm going to ride on his back for awhile!"

Toby was so happy, dog happy! He wiggled over all the attention they gave him. Then he walked over to Sir William and they touched noses for their greeting. Both knew each other.

Sir William nodded his head and he whinnied again. Oh! He was so happy!

All of them spent heavenly time, talked and had fellowship.

Angel Daniella asked, "Can we get together again with you?"

Wee Angel and Felicia agreed quickly, "Yes, we would love that!"

Felicia said, "We will have some very blessed times together. We can fellowship and do things together later!"

"Oh! We would love that!" agreed Daniella.

All of them flew up and off, Sir William. They enjoyed the moment. Angel Daniella went and picked a nice yellow rose and flew by, hovered and put it in the hair on Sir William's mane.

"There!" she said, "That's for you, Sir William!"

Sir William felt so pleased and horse humble. They were now combing his hair, and he loved it.

Within heaven's time, Wee Angel, Angel Gabriella, Angel Daniella, and Felicia, formed a circle and said prayers to the Lord.

Then they said their good days to each other, including Sir William and Toby.

Angel Daniella and Angel Gabriella flew on their way. They waved as they went their way.

Soon Sir William with Felicia on his back and Wee Angel on Toby's back were again headed along the golden way.

They walked again, and knew there was a lot of glories ahead of them.

They had seen these glories when Sir William had flown towards these mountains and hills.

After time, they got closer to this area. Wee Angel was enjoying her ride on the back of Toby.

Now Felicia said, "Wee Angel, I never knew light and glories were so much a part of heaven, yet I know the Bible talks about this.

"It is just that!" added Wee Angel, "Heaven is made up of tremendous light and glories. It's light that makes it all, yet God has so much of his waters here. Waters and heavenly light are so much a part of everything else. Also the orderliness of creation is so awesome. It is his creation."

They walked in the glories through the trees, which again were getting more golden in hues and color as they walked closer! They saw ahead through the trees, a waterfall from high above!

They again were in these lights of glories.

The golden pathway went only so close to the falls.

Above them in a horseshoe formed falls, the water gently came to the lower level where they were! It was a very huge waterfall. It was so wide and long and horseshoe shaped in form. They saw the top where it came from, way up high, in tremendous light.

They saw the edges of the mountain by it, amongst the light. When they were flying, they only saw light. Now they saw the edges to it, but mostly light. At the base of this huge long falls, a river formed and very pool-like waters. There was no rushing waters as on earth, just a huge lake of waters from this.

To the sides of the waters was light, which made up the sides or mountain-like sides. As one looked upward, at the base were flowers on the sides above the lake, that was formed from this.

About them were, and many of them, flowers! They were around this lake of waters, which was pure, golden, yet very aqua in colors.

"Oh so aqua!" said Wee Angel.

There was a pathway around the lake, and with time Wee Angel, Felicia, Toby, with Sir William left the area. Other saints were on this pathway too!

Some were with horses, some with winged horses too!

Then they walked with Sir William and Toby. In a short time, both Wee Angel and Felicia got on the back of Sir William and let him do the walking! Toby walked along side of Sir William.

Wee Angel said, "He needs that and he likes that."

So they rode on him for awhile along this lake.

The lavenders about this were so pretty! In this area, the fragrance was awesome and the shores were filled with these plants. Both flew off Sir William and picked some lavenders, and smelled their beautiful fragrance.

Even Toby flew to where Felicia and Wee Angel were picking lavenders.

Felicia said, "Oh he flies so nice! As big as he is, he flies so graceful!"

"I do agree!" Wee Angel spoke as she flew back towards Sir William.

Soon they were on their way again!

Hedges were bordered with lavenders, rhododendron and many different colored flowers.

The heavenly land was very level around the lake. There were trees also that formed hedge-like rows along the lakeshore.

There were also some very beautiful fir trees ahead of them as Wee Angel, and Felicia, rode on Sir William. Toby ran and walked about, enjoyed everything.

They were headed on the golden path around the falls and the lake.

Daniel Leske

Chapter 3

A Time to Pray and Praise

They walked along the lake's shoreline on the golden pathway. Both Felicia and Wee Angel were totally in heavenly awe of their surroundings.

They again sang songs to praise God and they felt so much love of all things.

They enjoyed the glories of the area. They enjoyed these beautiful trees that God had created special for the lake.

"Felicia," Wee Angel said, "God created everything so special for each area."

They looked at the beauty of the falls and it's surroundings. The lake was very serene with ducks, and geese on it, even a swan or two!

As they rode on Sir William, many thoughts went through their minds. All were heavenly thoughts!

The lake went on as far as they could see, along with the shoreline. The heavenly lands were fairly level by the lake except by the falls, and there were some gentle hills as one looked far away from the lake.

As they rode, they were amongst hedges that went away from the waters and were in the trees by the golden way.

Ahead, the glories were above the trees and were stronger! Wee Angel knew, and Felicia soon knew why!

There was a grazing area for the horses. They got off of Sir William and left him there with Toby. The other horses enjoyed both, Toby and Sir William.

Felicia and Wee Angel walked and followed another golden pathway. Wee Angel did the directing and soon they were at another prayer area. It was hedged all around the sides. It was very park-like with the beautiful lilacs and rhododendrons around the area. The prayer area was open and very open to the lake. It was large, but just right!

They saw in the short distance the mighty waterfall at the edge of the lake from where they came and all it's glories above it.

There were other saints there in prayer, again some angels were above and in praise!

Both Wee Angel and Felicia took time to pray and praise the Lord. The heavenly prayer areas were always so filled with the Lord's holy presence. Special! These were special to God, special to the saints, and the angels.

Once away from the entrance, they headed back to Sir William and Toby. They talked with some of the saints on the way.

They walked with Felicia and Wee Angel to Sir William and Toby, and gave them a few hugs. There were a couple of other horses, and a couple of winged horses there too! They grazed, and waited for their passengers, the saints!

They said their good days! Felicia and Wee Angel flew on the back of Sir William. They walked on again around this lake that was fairly wide. They could see the other side. It was about the width of the falls, because the falls was so very wide.

Sir William walked on and on and on around this lake.

Wee Angel and Felicia had Sir William walk over to the shoreline, and from there they still could see the higher hills with the falls in the distance.

"It's so awesome!" Felicia said. "I feel so wonderful and blessed!"

"So do I, Felicia! So do I." answered Wee Angel, "We are going to head to another falls."

Sir William kept walking and soon the pathway went further away from the lake back into some hills, still with trees. He walked around the hills farther away from the lake.

As Toby followed along, sometimes he just had to fly a little. Toby flew up and around Sir William who would nod his head!

Then, from the golden hillside, there was a huge opening in the trees on a hill.

They saw that the lake had more falls from it.

All about the same height, but it had several separate rivers below the lake.

"There are four rivers." said Wee Angel.

These rivers flowed through the hills, and on to the lands of heaven.

They were beautiful hills that separated the lake forming the falls and the rivers. These hills were all flowered, just flowers on them, and they were between the rivers and the falls.

The falls were not real high, just beautiful! So peaceful! They noticed some angels flying above the rivers, fairly close to the falls.

They walked besides Sir William and Toby. They followed the golden way. It was in the hills and trees, yet it was somewhat at a distance, but along one of the rivers. They followed it for a distance.

Then Wee Angel said to Felicia, "We are going to get on Sir William again, and he's going to fly on, again to another place."

So up they flew onto the back of Sir William and up in the beautiful heaven's skies, he flew! Of course, Toby flew beside Sir William. There, they saw the beautiful falls, rivers, and hills with flowers.

Sir William and Toby flew on!

They praised God and for all he's done and thanked him for it.

Daniel Leske

Chapter 4

Sir William, Always Faithful

Sir William flew across the rivers, then more trees, more hills, more fields.

Toby flew along too! He wasn't able to fly high speeds like Sir William, but for this he was alright!

As they flew, other saints on winged horses joined in with Wee Angel and Felicia on Sir William.

Sometimes there were up to seven winged horses with saints on them. What a beautiful sight as they flew across these lands in the heavenly skies. They would travel with them, then they were on their way.

In time, Sir William with Toby approached another mountain range.

They landed at the base or in the hills on the golden path that went up into the mountains. Wee Angel and Felicia stood and looked all around the area. They noticed a couple of fruit trees nearby and walked over to them.

Eat again! They did! Both enjoyed every bite of this heavenly fruit that wasn't or had been on earth, as Wee Angel told this to Felicia. This was a time when they gave some attention to both Toby and Sir William. They ate for some time and talked with them that passed by on the path. Then, they walked along side of Sir William more up into the hills. Sometimes, Wee Angel and Felicia took their turns at riding on Toby's back.

"He doesn't seem to mind it!" said Felicia.

"Oh! He loves it!" added Wee Angel.

They were in an area where the hills were getting much steeper as they walked through them. They were going more upwards again!

There was a grouping of olive trees alongside the golden pathway, in fact, as they walked on the hills, soon everything was covered with olive trees. The mountains were still ahead of them.

They walked on upwards, through groves of olive trees, with nice big olives on them!

Of course, they had to have some and they enjoyed them!

There were small bushes amongst them, flowers, and beautiful grass that carpeted everything under the trees.

As they walked on, the slopes of the mountains started and soon they were through the olive trees. The mountainsides were pretty steep on both sides of the golden way.

Felicia said, "Wee Angel, it's always nice seeing the olives, like we did, and they tasted so good!"

Wee Angel added, "They did! Didn't they!"

Both took a little time and flew around Sir William. They gave him another big hug, then flew off the path, looked at some beautiful violets or mountain flowers that were on the slopes.

Toby ran after them, enjoyed every moment.

They picked some flowers and placed some in Sir William's mane. He seemed to enjoy it.

They walked on, upwards!

Wee Angel said, "I know where we are going, and it's again special."

The mountains were steep enough, so there were no trees, but there were bushes.

They walked and flew some, higher and higher, then they flew to the top of the range and it leveled as they flew along!

Soon there were some fruit trees. There were tangerines; also grape vines were there.

So they had grapes as well, and then ahead of them in the distance, they again saw glories above the mountains.

There were some other golden paths that joined theirs and headed in the same direction. On them were more saints and horses with saints. Above them flew more and more angels, headed the same way. The glories were beautiful.

"We are going to another special area for services and worship that goes on continuously! We'll stay awhile and then go on!" said Wee Angel.

So they walked with others and pretty soon there were some grazing lands for the horses.

There were some open areas with sheep grazing and many of them. There were also some cattle, grazing with the sheep. There were deer, even a few buffalo, and other animals of heaven, that were not on earth.

It was a pleasant sight to see for everyone.

Birds flew about as well! Heavenly glories were there. They left Sir William who grazed with other horses. Toby stayed with Sir William and the other horses. Toby loved it, and so did the other horses.

They talked with several smaller angels, just a little bigger than Wee Angel. They introduced themselves! There were Angel Jonathan, Angel Aaron, Angel Julia, and Angel Mila.

Of course, they flew about, flew over the sheep, some cattle, and other animals, then back by Sir William, Toby and the other horses. They said their good days to Wee Angel and Felicia. Then they flew to the services.

Daniel Leske

Chapter 5

Mountain Rim Sanctuary

They soon saw ahead of them the glories at the entrance. There were flowers to both sides.

Then as they approached the sanctuary, they could see everything better!

Along the sides, they saw angels hovering in the heavenly skies above the mountain's rim.

Everything was in order.

As they approached they heard the playing of instruments, the singing, and many voices, the praises of saints, and the hallelujah's to the Lord. All this they heard!

Heaven was alive! They walked closer along and on the top of the mountain to this open sky sanctuary.

Soon they saw the sanctuary inside the sides of the mountain or steep hillsides.

"It's like a valley filled with singers and angels all along the sides." said Felicia.

"That's exactly about what it is!" added Wee Angel.

They were at the main entrance. The area was like a valley, horseshoe shaped, that was open to the open lands of heaven on the far side.

The platform for the service was more to the center, much lower than where they were on the rim of the high side.

There were levels around the valley and in the levels, special areas, molded into the hills. This is where the saints would sit!

So you had groupings of saints all around, because the mountain hillside was there too with flowers on the sides of the hillsides between the groupings of the saints. These were flowered ridges that were between the different groups.

One saw a lot of ridges, with flowers, even smaller shrubs and bushes with flowers.

Stairways, all around the horseshoe shaped open-air sanctuary in the mountains. The valley opened up to the lands, which were small hills and further away flowers, trees, and streams.

They saw a couple of beautiful large streams amongst the hills in the open end of the sanctuary.

Above them were many glories!

Felicia said, "The music, the mighty praises, are so beautiful!"

Along the rim in the various sections were angels with trumpets, saints with trumpets, and brass instruments. They would play a mighty alter song and during it, praised the Lord. The saints came and went, stayed as long as they wanted too for this.

Prayer and worship were a part of it. The service was continuous! It went on and on!

Both Wee Angel and Felicia found a section on the upper rim to praise the Lord and worship him.

They spent some time there, thanked the Lord and praised him.

Above the rim, angel choirs sang with this. The glories were to all the sides. The light was beaming!

With heavenly time, Felicia and Wee Angel walked back out and were soon with Sir William and Toby. They loved their time there.

"It's so beautiful, how the Lord created these areas or lands so perfect so we can praise him." Felicia said.

"He's wonderful!" added Wee Angel as both listened to the praises.

Soon they walked to areas of the lower mountains.

They were so happy to have Toby with them!

They were still in the mountains, yet in the lower valleys of the area. They took another golden pathway and were in more hills, fairly high, and with trees.

Both took some time to pay attention to Sir William and Toby. So they rested along the way by a small stream that flowed through the mountain hillside.

There were beautiful shrubs!

They enjoyed everything, including Sir William and Toby.

Wee Angel and Felicia combed their hair. Sir William and Toby loved it!

They praised the Lord, thanked him for his presence, the glories, meeting many saints, and his creation.

Daniel Leske

Chapter 6

Gloria

As they rested, Wee Angel noticed a pond on the stream.

"Look!" said Wee Angel to Felicia, "Look at the pelican in the pond. I know her."

Wee Angel flew over to the pond, a big pond in a wooded area.

She flew up to Gloria. Soon both flew back and landed next to Felicia.

"That's a big pelican." said Felicia as she hugged her.

Wee Angel said, "Gloria is her name and she will come with us for awhile!"

So Felicia talked to Gloria as she enjoyed the attention.

Then Gloria flew up on the back of Sir William who also enjoyed the attention.

"I'm happy she is with us." added Felicia.

"Me too!" said Wee Angel.

Both smiled with excitement! Gloria flew and landed on Toby, then after a little time flew back onto Sir William's back.

Felicia was all smiles, "She's neat!"

Other birds flew close by and looked at Gloria as they usually did with her.

They walked to the lower hills and into groupings of orchard trees. They talked for a while!

Wee Angel said, "I remember some of the ideas Daniel and you had for children, the ideas of different dolls and teddy bears for the children."

"I looked at some flowers here and remembered that!" added Wee Angel.

Felicia said, "We did! We had beautiful ideas on bears and dolls. The Lord gave us those ideas!"

Gloria flew again unto Toby's back.

Wee Angel and Felicia flew up on the back of Sir William. He walked on and on and on.........., along the golden path, amongst many ponds, flowered areas, special groupings of trees and fruit trees.

They followed this path along another stream from the mountains. They went again along and in the hills at the base of the mountains with openness to the one side.

Ahead of them in the heavenly sky again were many glories!

Then after a time, the heavenly land was all level, but ahead were extremely tall trees with extremely large trunks similar to the redwoods on earth.

A stream flowed from between these trees and then flowed into the one that they were walking close to!

They walked into a very special area with trees, flowers and small stream size waterfalls beneath them.

Special rock formations were there. It was a beautiful sight as one looked at Sir William with Wee Angel on him, and Toby with Gloria on his back.

Ahead of them the glories of the forest were getting brighter and brighter again! There were paths going to other directions. This was common in heaven. Golden paths and golden walkways with golden ways on and off into other areas so the saints could go anywhere.

Then as Sir William walked on, the trees were getting closer together.

Felicia said, "Look ahead, Wee Angel, the trees are all in these glories and looking more like a gateway."

Wee Angel said, "Remember the trees and flowers are like those on earth, but yet different in what they are made of here in heaven. These are just a little more beautiful than earth's. It seems they are just a lot more glowing in their colors. More vibrant!"

There were hedges of flowers. There were rows and rows of rhododendrons. The base of the trees and streams flowed to and away from this entrance ahead of them.

Wee Angel said, "We'll put Sir William and Toby over there by the other horses. Gloria will stay with them. She'll stay with them as we go through the glory light gateway."

Sir William walked to the area and seemed to know some of the horses. Both horses and winged horses were there. An angel came to them. She said her name was Angel Rebecca, and that she would be going with them through the gateway. Wee Angel and Felicia loved that and thanked her. They were smiling and ready to be guided as both gave her a big hug.

Off they went through this gateway between the trees with many flowers.

Sir William, Toby and Gloria waited on the grazing land amongst the hedges for them.

Chapter 7

Through Another Gateway

Wee Angel and Felicia walked with Angel Rebecca through the lighted glorious gateway of trees and hedges.

They walked on the golden way where the golden light made the trees look more like light than trees. The light was getting awesome!

Angel Rebecca said, "We're going to fly upwards now!"

So all flew up and into more glories of light as they flew on and on in this light.

There were no more trees to their sides or heavenly lands. They flew in all light with Angel Rebecca.

On and on and on and on and on.........., they went in this light. Soon after, a heavenly time, the light lessened around them. They saw another mansion by the Creator as they neared the gateway. Soon out from the light into the heavenly mansion.

They soon landed and looked at what was there.

They knew they were in another city or city-like mansion in heaven. As soon as they had landed Angel Rebecca said to Wee Angel and Felicia, "I'll be with you this whole time."

Angel Rebecca had long brown hair.

Wee Angel said, "We thank you, Rebecca."

They rested on a special bench of gems close to this golden street that overlooked this city.

For now, Wee Angel and Felicia talked with Angel Rebecca.

"Can we hug you?" asked Felicia.

"I would love that!" she answered.

Both gave Angel Rebecca hugs and more hugs.

There was something very special about Angel Rebecca. They just knew it and felt it. They liked being with her.

They rested for a short time. As they looked, they were filled with awe. The street was beautiful and very golden. They were on the high side of a city that was off in the distance as they were on top of a high hill that was flat in their area. They looked out over the city.

"We are in another mansion of heaven." said Wee Angel.

They saw many lights, beautiful lights, and glories of light.

To their backside and high above them were more pinnacles of light. These were pinnacles, yet like different colored lights.

Felicia said, "The pinnacles are solid colored. One is one color and another a different color."

They were beautiful reds, oranges, rose, soft pinks. They looked at the pinnacles that were high above, yet went to the horizon away from them.

The entrance, they came through was all glories of light.

Angel Rebecca said, "We'll be going back out the same way."

In the distance on the horizon, there were glories that arched like a rainbow from the far left of the city to the far right, up and over, and above the pinnacles.

All in colors like the rainbow, but this was all light beams.

Again, as they looked at the city, there were levels to it.

It was very celestial. There was a definite openness to everything there.

They watched saints that were on the streets. They watched the angels that flew along the streets and flew towards the city.

There were separate mansions in the city too! They were within the light as they looked, yet they couldn't see everything because the light was so strong!

Felicia said, "It's like the mansion is hanging in space, because you can't see anything holding it, except itself."

It was so wonderfully celestial! Very open, and as they looked, the light was over and around everything. The light passed through things such as the benches. So golden and white! A lot of white to everything, but not a cloud, but yet clouds of light.

Even where they sat the area was open! A lot of gems made up everything around them.

Wee Angel and Felicia talked with Angel Rebecca. They gazed and looked with awe at the vastness of one of heaven's celestial cities. Soon they all agreed to go to another place, one of the mansions in heaven.

Chapter 8

A Special Mansion

They walked for a distance to the entrance through the gate into the glories of light, and again they flew fairly straight ahead into this light.

Angel Rebecca said they were going to another mansion.

"It's what I do!" she said to Wee angel and Felicia.

They flew, and flew, and flew, and flew, and flew... in the light.

They just knew that no matter what, they were alright and so they flew on!

Soon they saw ahead the light was lessening and a heavenly mansion was ahead of them.

Through the gateway of light, then into the open area of the next mansion. They landed on another golden street. They walked again to benches made from gems and they just had to look around at everything.

"These places are so beautiful." said Felicia.

"Isn't that what the Lord said about this." answered Wee Angel.

Angel Rebecca said, "Our Creator is always creating new and wonderful places for his own. For us!"

High above, amidst the light, in the distance from where they stood, was another falls. They saw falls of water and again, light!

There was a falls then celestial-like light, then another falls, then light, then another falls, all around them.

The waters came from high above and went slowly to the next level, which was below them.

They saw above the falls were light-like fires glowing and the blueness of the open skies. Above the skies, more light, circled about the blues of the sky.

Many waterfalls or light-like waterfalls with glowing hues. Twenty to thirty falls or more as Wee Angel or Felicia tried to count them. They were all from the same height. All went to the same level below them.

Behind them or towards the entrance were more mansions.

Mansions and open mansions with gems, made up the sides and open areas.

Glorious light emanated from the mansions that were there.

Angels flew and sang praises! Praises given to God the Father. There were heavenly sounds to the Father there.

Again, saints were there. Wee Angel, Felicia and Angel Rebecca talked to some of them.

Some smaller angels came by, still bigger than Wee Angel as always! Wee Angel was just used to it. They talked with them.

There were others that came and went into the entrance to another place in heaven.

After all their good days, Wee Angel, Angel Rebecca, and Felicia walked again through the entrance of light from the street. Then it was all light as they flew to another mansion in heaven.

They again flew on, and on, and on... !

After heavenly time the light was lessening! The light was less, but the sounds of praises were getting stronger and stronger!

They heard hallelujahs, mighty singing, mighty praises and, many voices that spoke together, "Praise to our Lord! Praise to our Creator! Praise to you, Father! We praise you! We worship you! We love you! We praise you!"

The voices got stronger as they flew and the light continued to lessen! Soon they were in a very white like, yet golden area with angels all around them.

Daniel Leske

Chapter 9

Awesome

Wee Angel and Felicia went up to Angel Rebecca and gave her a big hug!

"Thank you, Angel Rebecca for bringing us here and for being with us!" spoke Felicia.

Their heavenly eyes were awed!

It was like everything around them, to the side, high above, as far as their eyes could see, were angels singing, and saints singing!

Praises being given to the Father, "Hallelujahs!"

On and on and on!

Thousands and thousands and thousands of angels, praising God.

There were also many saints there as well!

It was like they were in a mansion close to his heart. Maybe, even on the mountain above God's city. They felt that it was like a court yard fairly close to the throne. It seemed like it was on one of the sides of his mighty mountain as they viewed everything. It was so holy!

"Angels! Angels! Angels!" Wee Angel said.

"And saints!" she went on!

The singing! The praises!

Everyone lifted their arms and praised him.

Wee Angel, Felicia, and Angel Rebecca lifted their arms and praised him.

Mighty sounds of instruments were all around them. Glories of light streamed high above!

The worship area of golden gems lit up the sky above!

Angels hovered high above, and upward! The angels were present in the light and cloud-like areas of white light.

Felicia said, "It's like a mansion room of just praises to the Father and seems close to or around the high mountain from the city."

"It is that!" answered Wee Angel.

"It's like a part of his throne area and mountain, above his mighty heavenly city!" answered Angel Rebecca.

They took more time to praise him. They lifted up their arms and praised him and sang to him.

As the three praised the Lord, a couple of angels came by them. They stood together in a circle, holding hands, then prayed, and thanked the Lord for being the blessing he was to them.

Felicia, Angel Rebecca, and Wee Angel, after heavenly time walked to the entrance of light to go on to another place. They walked and then they flew in the glories of the light. After heavenly time again the light was lessening! They flew through the entrance, and soon they saw they were again in a very open area.

They were back at the entrance of the forest and trees. They flew and landed on their feet on the heavenly grounds. They were back where they had started with Angel Rebecca.

Felicia and Wee Angel visited with her. Soon they were next to and by Sir William, Toby and Gloria who was on Sir William's back.

Angel Rebecca gave Sir William, Toby and Gloria hugs. Sir William and Toby loved the attention. Wee Angel and Felicia gave hugs as well! Then Angel Rebecca hugged them. They fellowshipped, prayed, and thanked the Lord for all they had seen on their journey.

They prepared Sir William for his journey.

They said their good days and soon Wee Angel, Felicia, Toby, along with Gloria on Sir William, walked from the area on the golden path.

Angel Rebecca walked back towards the entrance.

After a time, Wee Angel said, "We're going on to a couple of places and then we will be headed back to the Lord's city."

"Oh, Wee Angel what a beautiful journey, this has been for us." with joy in her heart, Felicia spoke!

"There will be more!" added Wee Angel.

Soon Sir William opened his mighty wings and he flew upward above the trees over the lands with Felicia and Wee Angel on his back.

Sir William flew upward and he flew faster again along the mountains. This was a little more challenging to Toby, but Sir William always slowed up for him when he got a little behind them. Gloria flew along side of them.

They flew over meadows, different fields of flowers. They also flew over some areas that had more tropical-like plants and trees below them.

Soon the mountains were more like hills.

Then Felicia looked ahead and finally said, "Look on the horizon, Wee Angel, look!"

There on the horizon, as far as their heavenly eyes could see, they saw waters.

"It is what it is!" said Wee angel. "It's a large body of water and a lot of it. We do have a lot of water here in heaven too!"

Onward, Sir William, Gloria, and Toby flew towards the edge.

"How large is it?" asked Felicia.

"That I don't know, Felicia." answered Wee Angel. "I only know it's a large body of water. It's very open here. Goes way, way, away in both directions and then curves outward and around!"

Sir William came to the water's edge and there he landed on the shore.

Gloria flew and landed in the waters. Soon Wee Angel and Felicia were beside him and looked out at the large body of water.

Chapter 10

The Aqua Sea

As Wee Angel and Felicia looked at the waters of heaven, they were so very beautiful in color, pure water.

Wee Angel said to Felicia, "This is called The Aqua Sea. You know God always said to me many times, "Water is so very special to me, my little one. My kingdom and earth are so dependent on it. The water makes them so special, my water!' Then he would say how pure the heavenly waters are and how wonderful the waters are on earth. God loves water. It's a big part of him, as is light."

Gloria the pelican was already in the water. She was so happy. She came out of the water and put her head by Wee Angel and Felicia. She made some sounds, and it was her way of saying she was going on, away from them.

"She's been so much fun to have with us." said Felicia.

Wee Angel quickly agreed, "One's friendship in heaven keeps building and building! It's what makes heaven so special."

Soon she flew out into the waters and was swimming along the shoreline enjoying God's heaven.

Wee Angel and Felicia were in the waters playing around Toby, and singing too!

The shoreline was very white in colors. The trees in the area were palm trees. There were also some hedges with very large flowers that bordered the palm trees and the beautiful vegetation, which included very large orchids under these trees.

Heaven's land in the area was fairly level, but they still could see mountains from where they had flown!

They saw hills with mountains in the distance. The waters had hills along the edges, and there were some leveled lands between the hills and the heavenly waters.

So beautiful and peaceful to them.

There was a golden way along it, and a special area of grass by it too!

They saw several saints in the area, also a few winged horses with passengers in the heavenly sky, just a short distance away from them.

Other birds of the waters like on earth flew above them.

Some saints on horses with wings passed by them on the golden way. A beautiful scene it was for all of them.

"I'm so happy, Wee Angel! I'm just so happy inside!" Felicia went on, "We've seen so much!"

Two saints, Bob and Dave paused and talked with Wee Angel and Felicia.

Of course, Sir William and Toby received some attention too!"

They saw a grouping of mango trees close by, all with fruit. They went and enjoyed some mangoes and even some bananas. They were there for quite some time and talked over many things.

They prayed, "Thank you, Lord, for everything!"

Then they flew up on Sir William's back. Wee Angel had him fly along the shoreline. A winged horse and a winged Bernard dog were a sight to see!

They flew along the golden way that went along the waters edge. On they went, and then he flew more inland.

They were on the other side of the mountain range they had followed before this. As he flew the mountains were closer to them and to their left side. Yet as Sir William and Toby flew along the mountain range, there were more and higher hills with trees in front of them.

Sir William flew over larger hills, around, through and outside the mountain range. Toby always let Sir William do the leading, as he flew beside or a little behind him.

Wee Angel and Felicia were overwhelmed by all they had seen and the love of it. Both were having so much joy. On they flew!

The trees below them were pine-like trees. Many of these were like the cedar trees on earth, only much taller and bigger! They had left the area that had been palm trees and the vegetation.

Then there was a ridge of hills. They flew up and over to the other side, still along the range to their left side.

As Sir William and Toby flew along, Wee Angel and Felicia saw ahead of them a special heavenly land.

Chapter 11

Winged Horses

"Look Wee Angel!" Felicia said, "Look at the winged horses."

There in the valley below them grazed these horses on the heavenly lands.

Ahead of them, in the distance was another ridge of hills.

There was a lot of glories above the ridge of the hills close to the mountains. They were so beautiful!

In between was a beautiful valley with hundred of horses.

Onward Sir William flew along the ridge towards the valley of horses.

Over pine-like trees and many cedar trees, Sir William flew, and soon they were within range of them. Toby as well flew along!

"Felicia! Look! They are all winged horses. Aren't they beautiful!" said Wee Angel.

Sir William was getting horsely emotional over it. He knew they were of his own kind.

Hundreds of them on these grazing lands of beautiful grass, surrounded by hills and many hedges, with some streams, and flowers.

Along the hills were more golden paths of heaven.

Sir William and Toby soon were close to them.

Wee Angel saw the horses more closely, "They are all winged horses."

"Wee Angel, there's grays, there's browns, there were many horses of different colors, but most of all white horses with wings." said Felicia. "How beautiful!"

"Yes, mostly white horses, like Sir William." finished Wee Angel.

Of course, here Sir William wanted his way, so he flew and set his hoofs right amongst them on some beautiful green grass.

The horses loved it, and so did Sir William. Wee Angel flew from his back, and got a rose quickly from a nice big rose bush filled with roses, and put it on his mane.

"Felicia, I sure don't want him to get mixed up with the other horses." said Wee Angel as she put the rose on his mane.

Then they flew around the horses, and they enjoyed the moment! As big as Toby was, he had no problems in fitting in with the horses.

He loved them.

They loved him.

Sir William grazed with them. Wee Angel and Felicia walked and gave attention to many of the horses and spent some time there.

The horses enjoyed the attention they received by them. Both flew onto the backs of several of the winged horses.

Some kept a distance, but many of the horses came closer to visit and see them.

Then after heavenly time, Felicia and Wee Angel flew on Sir William's back. Toby was ready to fly again! They were soon in the heavenly sky above these beautiful animals of the Lord's. Sir William and Toby flew towards the ridge of the hills ahead of them.

Soon, alongside, over and through to the higher hills, they headed in the direction of the mountains.

Then as they got closer to the mountains, Wee Angel had Sir William land, Toby followed, onto a grazing area by a golden path that was winding close and along the top of the ridge of these hills.

Again they saw through some of the trees, the beautiful winged horses.

There were beautiful maple, oak, walnut, and more fruit trees!

Wee Angel said, "We are going to walk from here toward the glories, that we've been seeing from the other ridge."

They walked on toward the mountain where they saw these glories going up and away into the heavenly sky. They enjoyed the hills, the flowers, and the trees.

There were also mountain flowers and azaleas along the way.

They loved this time to walk, pray, and praise the Lord. Both prayed, lifted their arms to God and thanked him for everything.

They talked with some saints and some angels.

Then ahead, they saw something special, along the golden way. They left Toby with Sir William, who grazed in a special area. The something special was a place of prayer in these hills amongst the trees, beautiful flowers, and under the glories of these mountains. The trees around the prayer area were many tall cedars. They were beautiful and tall!

The glories were so beautiful here.

Wee Angel and Felicia left Sir William and walked on another golden way amongst the trees to this special place to pray and praise the Lord.

Chapter 12

A Gateway and Prayer Area

Both their hearts were stirred; this was not new for Felicia and Wee Angel!

They walked on towards this prayer area on top of a hill and below the mountains, yet a part of the glories of the special gateway.

They entered the prayer area. They were so full of joy.

They knew they had been a part of the Creator's master plan. They found a quiet area there as the other saints prayed! They found a cushion type seat of woods and some little flowers on it.

Besides the bench were some reddish with purple, white roses.

They took a seat and reflected just a little on everything.

Felicia said, "I'm so thankful for the Creator, the one who said he would keep going and make mansions. He promised and said it so nicely, that he wanted a people for himself. He would have mansions, and he would provide for us."

Wee Angel listened and answered, "He's always been that way, Felicia. The angels love the Lord so much, love the saints, and do what he asks! He is God over all!"

Both listened to the prayers around them and saw saints kneeling by benches. Some were laying flat on the carpet-like grass with flowers in this special prayer area.

Some with arms uplifted! Angels hovered above and up in the glories toward the mountain. Outside the prayer area, Wee Angel and Felicia could not see the angels. Inside the prayer area, they saw angels high above in the lights, and some in white glories.

Felicia said, "They look like white glories, yet a little like a cloud, a combination of both."

Wee Angel agreed as she raised her arms, "Look way up there at the white glories. It looks like a cloud with angels, Felicia. Aren't they beautiful?"

Both looked!

They looked at the hedges and beautiful flowers on the edges of the prayer area.

They also enjoyed the beauty of the cedars outside the hedges.

The prayer area wasn't real big, it was fairly small for even a prayer area. Some prayer areas were extremely large, while this one small and very pleasant to the angels and saints.

Within this area there still were angels with instruments of praise. Other angels sang praises, spoke prayers, spoke sometimes in a heavenly language that only God knew!

Wee Angel said, "God, just likes it that way!"

Felicia said, "The Lord likes it that his own would speak that way on earth too!"

Those that spoke in an unknown tongue, that they realized, yet didn't understand, knew that the Lord understood it and that's all that matters!"

Felicia went on, "That way, God said he would be praised! So we lift hands and arms to praise him."

Then Wee Angel and Felicia lifted their hands and arms to praise the Father, the Creator of what they had seen and were a part of in heaven.

They slowly walked out and back to Sir William and Toby. Then on they went on the golden pathway and walked closer to the archway of glories on the top of the hills and by the mountains.

Wee Angel looked ahead and saw Angel Zechariah and Angel Aaron coming closer on the walkway.

Wee Angel said, "Felicia, Isn't it nice that Toby has been with us! Toby seemed to know them."

Felicia said, "Yes, it looks that way!"

Toby knew and ran towards them!

Wee Angel introduced the angels to Felicia and they were happy to see Toby again!

"We have been so blessed to have him with us!" Wee Angel spoke!

They talked awhile, then said their good days.

Toby wiggled all over, for they knew he was so happy.

Wee Angel said, "Toby, you'll be going with us, yet!"

Angel Zechariah flew, picked him a nice flower like a dahlia, and put it in Sir William's mane fairly close to his ears. He also put one in Toby's hair by his ears. They enjoyed that!

Sir William walked up to Toby and nodded gently to him.

Toby went, "Woof!" and Sir William whinnied!

Both were very happy over their little gifts.

Angel Zechariah and Angel Aaron took turns sitting on Sir William's back and then flew to the golden way. Soon they were on their way.

Wee Angel and Felicia were soon on their way with Sir William and Toby.

Chapter 13

Wings are Special

Wee Angel spoke to Felicia, "We are not going into the archway this time. We'll walk ahead and take another golden pathway to a lower level of the hills and the base of the mountains."

They took another path and slowly walked onward, with the glories above the trees, on the mountainsides, and hills.

Wee Angel said to Felicia, "Now look up into some of the glories. I wanted to show you something."

Felicia looked, "Oh my, Wee Angel! Saints walked upward on some heavier streams of light. Yet the streams of light moved upwards and they walked some! But from here, it looks like they are held up in heavenly sky glories by this bright light, intense light, and they still are walking too!"

Wee Angel added, "I wanted you to see they are going to a mansion like we did with wings. They are going to a beautiful mansion."

There was tremendous light about them. Now the light beams, are this way so one can't see them going up and down. One can only see the light glories. The Lord allowed you to see the saints going in these glories."

Wee Angel added, "Like the prayer areas where one can't see the angel's until you are in the prayer area, so it is with this. We can't see the saints going back and forth to the mansions. What we see are the glories that are about, up and away from the area into the heavenly skies."

She went on, "This makes this mountain and hill area so beautiful from a distance, helps make up the mountains, as well as a part of these mansions, which can be long distances away from here."

Felicia knew then that saints without wings still could get to some of the mansions, those with wings could get to more mansions.

Wee Angel said, "The wings are very special in heaven."

Felicia said, "I know that now! I'm so glad I got some wings. Thank you, Jesus."

Wee Angel went on, "The mansion could be close or very far away from the Lord's city. Remember heaven is vast! There is much to it!"

Both took some time to spend with Toby and Sir William. Both liked to have their hair combed!

Then, they walked to the base of the mountains. Saints came and went from the area. They talked with saints on six horses. They fellowshipped, talked, and prayed together.

Of course, Sir William was appreciated by the saints and even other horses. It seemed Toby got his share of attention.

They went on and on, as both were so exuberant, happy, and joyful!

They flew away from the golden path, as Sir William walked on!

They enjoyed the moment. They played, sat on some tree limbs, and ran some with Toby. Both enjoyed heaven.

In time, they were on more leveled land. Wee Angel and Felicia flew unto the back of Sir William. They put him into a gallop. Felicia loved it as Sir William galloped along side of them.

Soon some angels flew along side of them.

They were a little bigger than Wee Angel.

Angel Micah came too! Then Sir William slowed down to a walk so Angel Micah could talk to Felicia and Wee Angel and the three other angels.

He said, "You are to make your way back to the Lord's city. I'll meet you there!"

They talked a little, he left them and the three angels, flew on, bid them all good days.

Ahead of them was a lake along the mountain range. They were out of the hills and neared this beautiful lake along the mountains.

They took time to look at mountains and hills they came from, looked above, and saw a lot of glories up and away from there, as high as they could see, up into the heavenly sky.

The area had more glories, because of the archway, then the rest of the hills and mountains.

Yet, these glories were never as bright or gleamed like God's mountain and his city.

Chapter 14

Headed back to the Lord's City

They walked along the golden way at the base of the mountains and a large lake. They walked on the pathway with the lake on their right side, and the mountains on their left side.

On the four walked, enjoying everything about them. The area had beautiful trees, and again some of the most beautiful pine trees. Very rich in colors! There were some magnolia trees too!

The lake glistened and so sparkled in colors, with sparkles that seemed to dance from the waters, because of the glories in the heavenly skies above them.

Onward they went on the golden way. They enjoyed everything they could along the way. Sir William enjoyed it too! They even skipped for fun. This always was a time for Toby to play with them.

Then they flew some as Sir William trotted besides them. The winged horse could not take off anywhere, because of the length of his wings. It had to be a special area, an open area for him.

Within heavenly time, Wee Angel said, "See, ahead of us up in the mountains! It's another waterfall."

"It's so beautiful!" answered Felicia. They saw the falls high above. The mountains were extremely steep and almost straight upwards on the sides of the water. The mountains were the most golden colors in this area. The pines went high, along the base of the mountain. The golden way went towards the lake more, and the lake was further from the mountains. They looked and looked at it. It was a fairly wide waterfall, high up and looked like it came right out of the mountain itself as they viewed it.

Wee Angel said, "After this, we are going to fly pretty straight to the Lord's city to see Lord God. He wants to talk to us again and see how we are doing on everything."

"It's been just the most beautiful journey. Everything is so wonderful!" answered Felicia.

Wee Angel, Felicia, Sir William and Toby took another path, back along and towards the lake, as the shoreline was still along the mountain range, but the falls was further away from there.

They noticed some winged horses with some saints on them in the heavenly skies. Soon they came to more open lands so Sir William could open his mighty wings for flight.

Both flew on his back. Even Toby flew up behind Wee Angel and Felicia.

He did just fit on Sir William's back.

What a sight to see with Toby, Wee Angel, and Felicia on his back. He opened his wings and soon he was in the heavenly skies flying towards the Lord's city.

He flew along the shore, and then flew along the lake from the falls. It was a beautiful sight in heaven. Sir William with Wee Angel and Felicia and Toby. Other angels were in flight. Saints along the shore by the lake on winged horses, saints were on the walkways, with heavenly ducks and geese in the heavenly skies.

Beautiful pines too!

The mountain range was in both directions.

The water flowed, as it looked, right out of the mountain high above! Beautiful golden tones on the slopes, also mountain flowers were fairly high on the slopes.

They still saw the glories over the hills and mountains.

"They are so beautiful from here!" Felicia said to Wee Angel as Sir William flew onward above this special area.

It was a beautiful scene: the hills, the lake, the mountains, the waterfall, and the glories.

Sir William flew over and along the lakeshore and soon he was over more of heavens' lands.

He flew faster as he went to God's city. Toby seemed to love it!

He flew on and on and on!

In heaven's time, they saw the glories were getting stronger and stronger above God's city.

Even though the special areas had glories, there was no comparison to the glories above the city and around God's mountain.

It was superior to all other areas, both in intensity and colors of the heavenly skies. It provided all the light for heaven.

Chapter 15

Sir William Flew Onward

Sir William flew onward!

Sir William flew onward and onward!

The glories got brighter and brighter above them. Then in heaven's time, they saw the mountain and the city of the Lord's.

It covered the whole horizon ahead of them. Wee Angel knew the gate they were supposed to go to, by this city.

Wee Angel said to Felicia, "We are going to another gate and one you haven't been to yet!"

Sir William flew, and within time he eased up and soon they had landed in an open area with the gate in the distance from them.

Once they had landed, an angel flew from the Lord's city. Her name was Angel Hanna. She said they were to wait outside there and Angel Micah would soon be there.

She flew off back to God's city. The Lord's city was a short distance, but still a good walk to it.

They were on some very special open land off the pathway. Aside the golden way were two streams from God's city. These streams flowed along the way to the lands of heaven.

They could see some of the entrance or gate to the city from there. It was very golden, yet bluish in tones like blues into the golds.

There was radiance about the archway. Along side of the gate again were hedges, many hedges.

There were hedges with flowers around the open area. They noticed a place to sit by one of the hedges so Wee Angel and Felicia walked and sat on this bench. Sir William and Toby were close by them.

There was a special feeling about everything.

They were excited, jubilant, and they talked about this. Felicia and Wee Angel always loved to do that.

It didn't take long for the excitement to start for them.

Out from some olive trees, Tuddley Teddy and Annie came running towards them.

"Tuddley! Annie! Oh how wonderful!" spoke Felicia.

"Isn't it wonderful!" added Wee Angel.

Both ran towards Tuddley and Annie. They gave them the biggest hugs.

Tuddley and Annie were both wiggling with all their might.

They were so happy to see Felicia and Wee Angel again.

Both flew around and around them. They experienced every moment.

Tuddley and Annie said their "Hi's!" to Sir William and Toby.

All seemed to rejoice over their friendship.

For Felicia and Wee Angel their enjoyment wasn't just Tuddly, Toby, and Annie. It was everything they had and were apart of in heaven.

The golden road went upwards, slowly into God's city.

They were on the lower lands and there were flowers on both sides of the streams.

Outside the hedges, were many olive trees on both sides of the golden way and with hedges going out into the olive trees. The two rivers from God's city, divided into smaller streams that flowed out amongst the olive trees.

They couldn't see the archway, because of the trees, yet they could see the beautiful glories of God's mountain and city above the trees.

Three rows of olive trees were on each side between the golden path and the rivers, three more rows of olive trees, twelve rows in all.

Then some flower gardens, nicely spaced, then hedges started to the outside of these rows. Some of the hedges were made by cedar trees in a nice row.

Another golden path came from the main one into this open area.

Within heaven's time Angel Micah flew to Wee Angel and Felicia. They greeted each other.

He was going to wait with them as he told them, that the Lord's riders and horses were coming!

They talked, prayed together, and praised the Lord!

It wasn't too long and in the distance from across the lands, they saw many winged horses with riders flying closer towards them.

Daniel Leske

Chapter 16

The Riders and Horses

The riders and winged horses were fairly close now!

Angel Micah said, "Wee Angel and Felicia, there are 60 to 70 winged horses and with riders in this group. We'll stay where we are until they have all landed here."

The riders were getting more and more in single file as they flew closer to them.

The area was plenty open for all of them.

Soon the horses placed their hooves on heaven's land with riders, one at a time.

Then as they came in, the horse would fold it's wings and walk, forming a straight line. They formed two long lines, all, in perfect order, across the open way.

There they stayed! The riders got off their horses, very orderly, and stood beside them. A beautiful formation as Wee Angel and Felicia looked at them.

On each side of the golden path from the open area to the main golden path were two huge olive trees. One on each side of the path. Both were filled with many olives, a beautiful sight! Felicia said, "Look above, Wee Angel."

Wee Angel looked, "Look at all the angels flying above the trees."

On both sides of the golden way to God's city, angels hovered and were forming more and more rows above the trees, up and away from the golden road in lines towards the archway to God's city.

They had instruments in their hands. Others were already singing glories and praises to the Father.

The angels played sounds of welcome, honor, and glory! Trumpets started to sound! The glories of the city were stronger and brighter!

What sounds filled the heavenly skies.

"What a beautiful feeling!" Felicia added to Wee Angel.

Wee Angel nodded in agreement. She knew!

The angels kept playing and singing above!

Several flocks of doves flew over the open area above Wee Angel and Felicia. The power and light gained in strength about the horses and riders. All of heaven seemed to ring with praise and glory. God's city was very radiant with glories from it. The glories over the city were getting stronger!

Hallelujahs filled the heavenly skies.

By the olive trees, the light got brighter and brighter!

Soon walking from the golden path unto the other path between the two olive trees was Jesus with two disciples.

Angel Micah said to Felicia, "They are Matthew and Mark."

The three walked closer and were in conversation. Both Wee Angel, Felicia knelt, as well as Angel Micah and all the riders of the winged horses. They all knelt to his presence.

Chapter 17

Jesus
and
His Name for Sir William

Sir William and Toby stood close by Wee Angel and Felicia.

Jesus with Matthew and Mark walked forward to the leader of the riders. Jesus spoke to him. Jesus and the riders wore basically the same garments as before, but the garments were different in color. The riders colors were with the slacks, a light to medium blue trim and the outer half robe white with aqua trim. His garment was the same in color. Still, there were gems of light on his shoulders and sleeves. The gems on his garments and the riders were the same as before!

Matthew and Mark were clothed in white robes, but casual looking and fitting for the time.

It wasn't too long, Jesus with Matthew and Mark, walked towards Felicia, Wee Angel, Angel Micah, Toby, Tuddley, Annie and Sir William.

Jesus told them, they could stand up and he introduced Matthew and Mark, to Felicia.

Many hugs were given and they talked!

Felicia said, "I love you, Jesus. I waited a long time to meet you, Matthew and Mark."

Wee Angel then said, "I love you too, Jesus."

Both Wee Angel and Felicia had to hug Jesus again and again!

"My children! I love you both, so much!" Jesus had a little tear in his eye. The moment was precious.

Jesus walked close to and in front of Toby, Tuddley, and Annie.

The three seemed to stand in attention and honor of Jesus.

He said, "I see Wee Angel, you have been making good friends for Felicia with these special little ones!"

Tuddley, Toby and Annie stood in attention. They knew who Jesus was and is!

Jesus turned and talked more with Angel Micah.

The angels about them then played a familiar song from earth, "Turn your Eyes upon Jesus."

The sounds filled the heavenly air.

Angels sang the words. Little Felicia and Wee Angel joined into the singing as Jesus stood before them. The riders knelt yet!

There were now angels above the open area as well as along the golden way to God's city.

Angels flew around the sides of the open area, above the olive trees and up and away into the heavenly sky, high above in the glories.

It looked like hundreds and hundreds and hundreds of angels, flew and filled the heavens above them. Above and around so quickly!

Felicia was in wonderment over it all! How could they do that so quick, but they appeared so quickly to their heavenly eyes!

The angelic choir was above and around them. They continued with "Turn your Eyes upon Jesus." The angels knew about these horses and riders and the leader of them, and his name is JESUS!

"Thank you my children!" Jesus said again, "Thank you so much for loving me, caring and listening! You are special! Thank you for taking care of Revelation. I'm going with them so I'll be taking Revelation again!"

"Revelation!" said Felicia, "What a beautiful name for Sir William. What a powerful name! It does have a lot of meaning. Now I know what you were going to tell me, Wee Angel!"

Jesus and Wee Angel smiled.

Micah and Felicia smiled.

Everyone knew his importance!

Wee Angel and Felicia walked and gave Sir William a big hug! Quickly, Toby, Tuddley and Annie went by Sir William and put their heads up by his head. In their ways, they said their good days to him!

Felicia and Wee Angel knew they would be seeing Sir William again!

The light around Revelation got brighter and stronger.

"Can we do something before you go!" Both Wee Angel and Felicia spoke together."

Jesus said, "Absolutely!"

They flew quickly to some roses and they found some big red roses. They brought them and handed them to Jesus.

They loved to give Jesus roses.

He took them and held them by his heart, "Again thank you, Felicia and Wee Angel. Just know that I love you!"

Then Revelation followed Jesus, Mark and Matthew.

Angel Micah stayed with Felicia and Wee Angel.

Jesus took Revelation aside from the others, then the brightness of light grew mightily around Revelation so Wee Angel and Felicia couldn't even see them. Then as it lessened Revelation had a special beautiful saddle like before.

Jesus said good days to Matthew and Mark who then walked towards the golden road. Jesus spoke to the leader of the riders.

They mounted on these beautiful white winged horses that had tremendous power of light and more so!

They were ready to enter the heavenly skies.

Jesus commanded the leader who commanded the others and soon all were taking off one at a time. Last to leave was Revelation with Jesus on him.

He looked at Wee Angel, Felicia, and Angel Micah. Jesus nodded to them. Jesus spoke to Revelation and with power and gracefulness he was in the heavenly sky.

Jesus and Revelation were soon in the front of the formation of these riders on the beautiful white winged horses, headed across heaven.

Chapter 18

The Vision

They watched with much interest as Jesus and the riders left the area. They watched and they watched, as these mighty riders of the Lord's on winged horses went across the land of heaven.

There was a very powerful light around them and Wee Angel and Felicia knew what extreme power went with them.

"I'm with wonder as I watch this." said Felicia.

"We'll talk about that in a little while!" added Wee Angel.

Angel Micah stood between Wee Angel and Felicia with both his hands on their shoulders.

They just stood in total amazement!

The angels above the golden way and above the area were slowly leaving the area. Most flew towards the Lord's city and mighty mountain.

They watched the horses with Jesus, at times it looked like the brightness of the sun moving across the lands.

"What power is there!" added Wee Angel.

Angel Micah said, "There's more power there, than you'll ever know if they want to use it! Just know that my children. They are what they are!"

Soon they saw just light as they were in the distance.

Angel Micah said his good days to Wee Angel and Felicia.

He said, "Wee Angel, Lord God wants to see you as soon as you are finished here."

Wee Angel said, "We'll be heading there soon!"

Angel Micah gave them a hug and then flew towards God's city.

Wee Angel and Felicia talked a little!

Wee Angel said, "I want to share with you a little on the riders. Let's walk over by the olive trees."

They walked to the two large olive trees by the golden road. They soon sat on the rich grass under one of the two trees, with beautiful flowers by them.

The trees were bountiful, filled with olives!

Wee Angel continued, "Jesus and the riders on the white horses are very special. The Lord said to me, there is a time coming when there would be a special mission. I talked to you right after you got to heaven, about some of it."

She went on, "Now you see, Jesus with the white winged horses, would be used at earth in his time. That's part of what this is all about, but not yet! Felicia, I don't know when, only the Father knows, not even the riders. There will be a season on earth as the the Bible talks about, the season is when Jesus will use these horses and riders is more and more approaching! So much depends on earth."

She continued, "Just know Jesus is the commander-in-chief of everything in heaven and will know the time! At that time, Jesus and the riders will assemble with the mission of battle on earth. There will be an army of riders with horses. At that time, they will intervene to keep earth."

Wee Angel paused and went on, "There will be many armies on earth in battle and ready for more battle. Then as the battle unfolds, in that time, which is ahead yet, one doesn't know when! The heavens will open and Jesus with the winged white horses and riders will go through the heavenly skies and clouds to the horizon of earth. The sight of this will be awesome. The armies on earth will see all of this happen. Angels will be to the sides of Jesus and these riders. The Dove(Holy Spirit) will also be hovering by the side of the doorway to earth. Angel Michael, Angel Gabriel, Angel Micah and other powerful angels will be there to the sides holding open the doorway of heaven as these riders go through to earth. There will be thousands of angels to the sides of the riders on heaven's side as they come flying through the doorway!"

Wee Angel went on, "The armies will see the power of this. They will know Jesus is in command, dressed for battle if needed, army of riders behind him. There will be light like these armies on earth have never, ever seen before. They will know that their time is at hand."

Wee Angel continued, "The Bible speaks that a two edged sword will go from his mouth. It speaks of the clothing. One has to remember that Jesus is Light. The power of the light will be strong that if Jesus wills, then light rays of might and destruction like lightning will smite the armies on earth. This will come from his mouth meaning JESUS IS THE SOURCE OF ALL LIGHT and the greatest power of it.

At that time, the armies will know that heaven is for real. But it may be too late for them. They may fight! They may kneel!

They are totally at God's mercy, but his mercy might be gone because of what they have done to earth and the Lord's own."

Wee Angel finished, "It's not yet, Felicia! They just went on a ride about heaven, then they'll return and we'll have Sir William that is Revelation back with us.

Chapter 19

The Joy of Heaven

Both talked and Felicia knew in her heart a little about the coming times.

They knew it was best to leave Tuddley, Toby, and Annie there.

Wee Angel said, "We'll be back! We are going to see Lord God. I can't say enough for the beautiful times we have been having here."

Felicia added, "All of you, have been so good to us. Wee Angel and I love you, and we'll be back."

With that Wee Angel and Felicia hugged each one. Somehow, with everything that was happening, it was hard to fight back tears of joy in their friendships with them. Wee Angel and Felicia wiped away a few tears and soon were smiling, giggling as well! They enjoyed their friends.

There were a couple of angels close by, so Wee Angel asked them to take care of Annie, Toby and Tuddley until they returned from the city.

They walked from the grass under the olive tree and walked on the golden pathway towards God's city.

They walked with rows of olive trees on each side. They still had a distance to walk with streams and trees to both sides of the golden road.

Soon they saw more of the archway gate to God's city. They walked a little more upwards on the golden way.

Ahead of them and to the sides of the archway were waters, which flowed from God's city and mountain. They flowed on steps of gems. The river flowed over many, many steps made by gems on both sides. These came from along a wide street in God's city.

They had to go up some steps as well as they neared the archway of gems. This one had gems of light blue upon its sides with a lot of light that came from them.

There were flowers on some hedges, climbing flowers were along the rivers and special golden tones on the stairways.

To the sides were more waterfalls that flowed from streams above! On both sides were many small falls of water, which poured, into the rivers along the golden way. These went into the rivers, which flowed over many steps coming out of the city.

Angels hovered above the gate and high up like the other gates.

Angels sang praises, instruments played, to the Lord.

Wee Angel and Felicia walked and looked at everything in this glorious moment. They looked at the glories of God's city, sides of his mountains as well, and the beautiful gate to the Lord's city. This one was awesome too!

Felicia said, "Wee Angel, everything has been so beautiful! I'm so happy to be here.

Wee Angel added, "You and I have had some wonderful times and they are only starting in heavenly time!"

Again Felicia, "I made so many friends and meeting Jesus already! You and I had some beautiful moments with Sir William. There's so much to say about this winged horse and how he is so special!"

Felicia went on, "Then there's Tuddley Teddy. How he was with us and one could hug him so much! Annie, her presence was so kind and she was so nice to be with too! What a beautiful friend Toby has become for us. Then the other animals and birds as well!"

Felicia kept on, "We've been to many beautiful places."

Wee Angel said, "Felicia, there's many more, because heaven is so vast."

"I know that now!" answered Felicia.

They paused along the golden road. They looked at God's city, the rivers, mountain, olive trees, and hedges.

They both prayed!

Felicia prayed, "Thank you Lord for everything, for my friends, Jesus and Wee Angel, Angel Micah and the other angels.

Wee Angel added in prayer, "Thank you Lord for Felicia and the wonderful time you provided for us."

They stood and praised the Lord for all he does for everyone.

Felicia tried to hold her tears of joy, but they were there.

Wee Angel was in tears too! Both felt so blessed by the Lord. The moment spoke for itself. Their hearts were so full.

Felicia said softly, "I'm trying to put everything in order and contain all that we've seen and has happened!"

Both now had smiles on their faces. Smiles of joy and well being. They were having tears of joy, smiles of joy. Their hearts were full!

They were just about ready to walk on, when two angels came flying along the golden road to God's city.

As they flew closer, Wee Angel said, "It's Angel Gabriella and Angel Daniella!"

They landed by Felicia and Wee Angel with more greetings given to each other.

Angel Daniella said, "This is such a blessing that we can see you again!"

Wee Angel said, "Do you want to come wih us. We are going to see Lord God."

Immediately Angel Gabriella said, "Yes we would love to, thank you for asking!"

All of them flew to some flowers and picked some more roses and carried them.

"We'll take them to Lord God to give to him." Wee Angel said.

So they walked onward on the golden way. All four of them together! Wee Angel being just a little shorter.

There was Wee Angel, Felicia, Angel Daniella and Angel Gabriella.

They laughed some!

They cried some!

They smiled some!

They even giggled some!

All four walked on!

In their hearts was the joy of heaven as they headed into God's city.

Daniel Leske is available for speaking engagements and public appearances. For more information contact:

Daniel Leske
C/O Advantage Books
P.O. Box 160847
Altamonte Springs, FL 32716

info@ advbooks.com

Daniel has also published *The Joy of Heaven 1* and *The Joy of Heaven 2* available from *Advantage Books*

To purchase additional copies of this book or other books published by *Advantage Books* call our order number at:

407-788-3110 (Book Orders Only)

or visit our bookstore website at: www.advbookstore.com

We are planning to have some children's products of the characters from *The Joy of Heaven 1, 2,* and *3*. They would be stuffed animal toys, teddy bears, figurines, possibly dolls and other products. For more information:

www.thejoyofheaven.com

Facebook: Daniel Leske / Author

Advantage
BOOKS

Longwood, Florida, USA
"we bring dreams to life"™
www.advbookstore.com